Responding Faithfully to the Environmental Crisis

Christianity at the Time of the Anthropocene

Timothy Howles

Ordained Minister in the Church of England

Associate Research Fellow of
the William Temple Foundation

GROVE BOOKS LIMITED
RIDLEY HALL RD CAMBRIDGE CB3 9HU

Contents

Acknowledgments
With thanks to the Revd Margot Hodson and the Revd Mia Smith
for their comments during the editorial process.

First Impression January 2019
ISSN 1470–854X
ISBN 978 1 78827 071 7

Introduction

Pinned up on the noticeboard of a church I once visited was a laminated sheet of A4 paper. Its crumpled and dog-eared edges suggested it had been up there on the wall for many months or even years. Its title simply read: *10 Things Christians Must Do to Help the Environment*. This was followed by an itemized list of action points relating to composting, light bulbs and cycling to work.

It was hard to argue with any of its suggestions, which were all very practical and sensible. But at least one person in the congregation had evidently become dissatisfied with this notice! For stuck on the bottom was a Post-it note, written by hand in red ink, containing the following verse:

> Say to those with fearful hearts: 'Be strong, fear not! For see, your God will come and save you.' (Isa 35.4)

That notice, with its brief addendum, has remained in my mind ever since. I have always felt it conveys something of the dilemma facing Christians as we seek to respond faithfully to the contemporary environmental crisis. Quite rightly, the notice was appealing to the congregation to do something—hence its list of practical suggestions that we were all encouraged to follow. But evidently this had prompted a theological backlash of sorts from someone! And the verse from Isaiah that had been inserted, with its strong deferral to providence and its anticipation of the future action of God to make right the problems we have caused for ourselves here on Earth, seemed to contradict the urgent call to action being made in the original notice itself. Somehow, these two themes were not well integrated.

We all appreciate the severity of the threat posed to us (and to future generations) by the contemporary environmental crisis. But how should we respond? Are Christians called simply to faith and prayer at a time like this, while we wait for the liberation of the Earth from its bondage? Or is the priority to be action and engagement in the social, cultural and political arena, with the hope and expectation that we can change things for the better now? More importantly, is there a way of synchronizing these two, so that our faith in God to redeem and heal the world at the end of history might not be the cause of inertia or inaction, but rather the engine of a renewed engagement in the structures of contemporary society?

I will address these questions through the prism of a concept that most of us have probably heard of, but whose significance and usefulness might not have been immediately apparent to us before: *the Anthropocene*. Recently, references to the Anthropocene seem to be everywhere: we may have seen the word crop up in the news, on social media, or even on the placards of protesters at climate change events taking place in different cities around the world. The idea seems to have got people talking and, more importantly, it seems to have got people thinking. That is not surprising: the concept of the Anthropocene has a way of troubling some of the assumptions we have taken for granted up to now and of asking searching questions about how we ought to proceed in the future. In fact, I would go so far as to say that the concept of the Anthropocene forces us to re-evaluate who we are as human beings and how we relate to the world around us. And, on that front, Christianity must surely be part of the conversation.

Understanding the Anthropocene

So what is the Anthropocene? And how might the concept help us to frame a distinctively Christian response to the contemporary environmental crisis, one that might synchronize faith and action in a more productive way than we have managed up to now?

In what follows, I will attempt to answer these two questions. To begin with, I will introduce the concept of the Anthropocene, explaining what the term means and why it is useful for describing our current situation (chapter two). Thinking about the Anthropocene prompts us to ask important questions about responsibility: whose fault is it that we have ended up where we are? For some, religion is to blame for engendering attitudes towards the natural world that have led us to this point. On the contrary, I will suggest that its roots derive from modernity itself and especially from its secular ideology (chapter three). If this is true, then modern, Western societies must be self-critical about their response to the current crisis (chapter four). For example, it seems intuitive to many that the way forward will be found in the development of new technologies and engineering solutions to offset the effects of climate change. But to what degree is this simply replicating the mindset that led humanity into the Anthropocene in the first place? With this framework in place, I will begin to map out a distinctively Christian response. Evidently, as responsible members of society, there are many practical actions Christians can take, whether as individuals or in the context of our church communities. All such efforts are crucial. But there is something else Christians can offer too: an alternative story about the future (chapter five). This might be a contribution to the change of heart that global society as a whole needs to take if it is to slow down and reverse the effects of environmental change for ourselves and for future generations. Finally, I will explore in more detail the story that Christians need to tell at this time. I will consider some scriptural resources, perhaps even unexpected ones, that might aid us in this task (chapter six).

My aim throughout is not to undermine constructive approaches to the environmental crisis that are being pursued elsewhere. Many useful and necessary initiatives are currently underway, whether at a macro level (in the domain of intergovernmental co-operation, the response of businesses and industry, technological solutions, and so on) or at a micro level (actions being taken by individuals to address their local patterns of consumption and wastage of natural resources). But I do wish to suggest that a Christian ethical response can (and must) be added to this mix. For Christianity has something distinctive and vital to contribute to the discussion. And the unsettling, but very interesting, concept of the Anthropocene is one way of exploring what this might be.

> **Christianity has something distinctive to contribute to the discussion**

For further background on these issues, you might like to consult previous booklets in the series, in particular E184 (*An Introduction to Environmental Ethics*) and E177 (*The Ethics of Climatic Scepticism*).[1] This booklet can be profitably read in conjunction with them.

2   What is the Anthropocene and Why Does It Matter?

I wonder if you have ever heard of the Subcommission on Quaternary Stratigraphy? It consists of a small group of geologists, about thirty in total, who are engaged in the study of rock layers and layering.[2] Its publications are certainly niche. By the look of its website, it evidently does not expect to receive much attention from the public at large. And I must confess that I have not been in the habit of following its research output very closely.

Until recently. For there is at least one aspect of its work that should cause us to take note and pay attention. This rather obscure academic body has been given the task of investigating whether the Earth has entered a new geological epoch or not—and if so, on what date? Were this new epoch to be admitted, it would supersede the Holocene, the epoch in which we currently reside. Although this might sound like a rather specialized and eclectic matter, a great deal is actually riding on the decision. After all, the Holocene has been in place since the time of the last ice age, that is, for the last 12,000 years or so. It has provided the climatic conditions for the flourishing of all recorded human civilization, from BC to AD and right up to the present day. Hence, the Holocene is all we have ever known.

Has the Earth entered a new geological epoch?

And yet, this is the stable climatic situation we may be about to leave behind.

The proposal the group is considering is whether (or not) we have entered a new geological epoch to be called 'the Anthropocene.' This term is intended to convey an understanding of the Earth system as being primarily conditioned by the activity of the *anthropos*, that is, by human beings—you and me. In the Holocene, we understood the natural environment around us as having been shaped by various physical forces—ice, wind, rivers, floods, soil erosion, volcanoes, even the orbit of the planet around the sun. That ensured a certain degree of stability. But in the Anthropocene, this would no longer be the case. The principal definer of the natural environment around us would now be… us. As one academic survey puts it, to be in the Anthropocene would be to posit that human activity 'has become so large that it rivals some of the great forces of nature in its impact on the functioning of the Earth system.'[3] The impact and consequences of this shift are hard to predict. We do not really know what kind of disruptive feedback loops it will engender. We do not even know how long this situation will be sustainable for human existence on the planet. And so the stakes could hardly be much higher.

The formal announcement of the arrival of the Anthropocene has not yet been made. This is because, like any scientific discovery, it requires empirical justification. In this case, what is needed is stratigraphic evidence. The story of the Earth is marked out in layers of sedimentary rock underneath our feet, rather like the rings of a tree revealing its history and age. What geologists are looking for, then, is evidence of a layer deposited by the activity of human beings. This would provide confirmation that human activity has been of sufficient scale to warrant the designation of an entirely new geological epoch.

The alarming news is that such a layer is clearly present.

Dating the Anthropocene

What is more challenging is to date it, thereby demonstrating when the Anthropocene formally began. Some within the scientific community offer an 'early Anthropocene' hypothesis. First proposed by palaeoclimatologist William Ruddiman in 2003, this claims that farming activity and deforestation carried out by primitive human communities around 8,000 years ago, although relatively small-scale and localized compared with today, actually released sufficient methane and carbon dioxide into the atmosphere to alter global climatic conditions. (Ruddiman even suggests that this intervention probably forestalled an incipient ice age that would have begun around that time.) It was here, it is proposed, that the Earth system was sufficiently altered by human activity to warrant the beginning of a new geological epoch.[4] A more likely candidate, however, would be the arrival of the Industrial Revolution in Europe, with the development of factories and other large-scale, mechanized means of production that were associated with that event.[5] Some scientists argue for a more recent date still: perhaps the depositing of this layer can be traced to the accelerated burning of fossil fuels that has occurred in Western consumer societies from as recently as the 1990s.[6] The debate continues. And there must be sympathy for those charged with making this decision. After all, geologists are accustomed to handling large timescales. They usually think in terms of millions and billions of years. But here they are being asked to decide on a geological alteration that may have taken place as recently as…perhaps twenty years ago! Such are the strange times we find ourselves inhabiting.[7]

The Earth was sufficiently altered by human activity to warrant the naming of a new epoch

We may not have come across the work of the subcommission before. But we have almost certainly heard of the Anthropocene. The term is becoming more and more widespread. In the last year or two, references to the Anthropocene have been appearing frequently in the news.[8] Barely a week goes by without it cropping up in an article reporting on the effects of global environmental change.

Why has talk about the Anthropocene become so prevalent recently? Surely it is because the term encodes an observation we have all made for ourselves, namely, that there is **There is something out of balance in our relationship with the world around us** something out of balance in our relationship with the world around us. We have been living our lives as if the Earth was able to sustain a trajectory of endless growth and consumption. Our scientific and technological innovations have fooled us into thinking this could go on forever. But at the time of the Anthropocene that assumption becomes harder to sustain. The idea that we are inhabiting a planet that is simply there for us to use as we wish has been exploded. The patterns of behaviour we have adopted have caused the natural environment around us to be altered to such an extent that it has triggered nothing less than a new geological epoch! The natural world, which we thought was there to be deployed for our own needs, is now rising up against us and saying: *no more*. Will the Anthropocene be as conducive to our flourishing as the Holocene has been? Almost certainly not. We will have to find a new way of living on this Earth if we are to continue.

Living with Threat

In the popular book and film *The Life of Pi*, the protagonist finds himself stranded in the middle of the Pacific Ocean on a small lifeboat.[9] As it turns out, this is by no means a comfortable state of affairs, for alongside him on the boat is a large Bengal tiger. The young man has to learn (and learn quickly) how to occupy the same space as an animal that is powerful, untamed and hungry. Perhaps our situation is analogous? Once upon a time, we thought of nature as something that was locked away in its cage and firmly under our control. We supposed that we had the right to make it work for us. And we did not think too much about the consequences. But at the time of the Anthropocene, that situation has changed. The very nature that we thought was our servant is now to be found prowling around in our midst, refusing to be dominated, and threatening the very conditions of our survival. Some new settlement is required if we are to make the shared space of the Earth habitable for ourselves and for future generations.

If this is a suitable analogy for the situation that pertains at the time of the Anthropocene, then Christians will be interested to engage in the conversation. For this implies that many of the most cherished ideas of contemporary society are being put under strain. The worldview of modern, Western, secular people has assumed a trajectory of ever-increasing material progress. Through the efforts of science, engineering and technology, the message has been: *you can have more than you had before*! But the Anthropocene puts up a stop sign to all of this. The Earth itself is reminding us of its own planetary boundaries. And this is compelling us all to think in a new way.

3 How Did We Get Where We Are?

How did global humanity get to the point where (depending on the decision of the geologists) we find ourselves on the precipice of a new and entirely unpredictable planetary situation? What are the attitudes and ideas that have led us to the time of the Anthropocene?

For some, religion is to blame—and the Christian religion in particular! This argument derives from a famous article published in 1967 by the American medieval historian Lynn White entitled 'The Historical Roots of our Ecologic Crisis.'[10] White read the Genesis creation narratives as assigning to humanity the role of master over nature, having been granted dominion by God over its various forms of life. This, he argued, has caused human beings to understand themselves as elevated *above* the created world and hence as justified in deploying its resources at will for their own consumption. White suggested that this hegemonic attitude has manifested itself with different degrees of intensity throughout human history. But its origin is ultimately traceable to Christian doctrine. And so he concludes as follows:

> We shall continue to have a worsening ecological crisis until we reject the Christian axiom that nature has no reason for existence save to serve man.[11]

The argument of Lynn White is frequently cited in academic articles. And its influence on popular culture has been significant too.[12] Many people do think of religion (and often the Christian religion) as being in some way to blame for destructive human attitudes towards the natural world.

But a much more likely candidate can be identified. I would like to suggest that the attitudes and ideas that have led to the Anthropocene derive not from a Christian worldview, but from modernity itself, and especially from its secular ideology.

In order to test this thesis, we need to engage in a brief historical survey. In the medieval mind, there was no split between God, nature and human beings. People believed that the operation of the natural world, including the weather and climatic conditions, was directly under the control of a sovereign God. Human beings therefore thought of themselves as being embedded in the natural order of things as parts of a larger whole, a microcosm nested within a macrocosm.[13]

But with the advent of modernity in seventeenth century Europe that world-view began to change in subtle ways. Something shifted in the way human beings understood their relationship with the natural world around them. The roots of this shift are found in medieval nominalism, particularly the philosophical thought of William of Ockham, according to which there exists no sensible and perceptible correlation between the divine will and the unfolding of events here on Earth. This opened the door for the material world to be investigated independently of the theological symbolism that had previously prevailed. The natural sciences emerged, with their strictly empirical method. Mathematics became the arbiter of relations between material bodies. New discoveries about the functioning of the universe were made, especially through the work of Galileo. In all these developments, the key idea was that of mechanism: the realm of matter could now be measured and controlled by us because it was understood as operating in a regular and predictable way.[14] The hypothesis of a divine agent or agency determining everything from the movement of the planets to the falling of the spring rain was now rendered unnecessary. The link between providence and the operation of the cosmos had been severed.

Modernity as a Religious Ideology

The French sociologist Bruno Latour has offered an interesting proposal about this story.[15] Although it is clear that modernity represents a rupture with the religious worldview that had prevailed before, Latour nevertheless argues that modernity itself represents a kind of religious ideology. On the one hand, to be modern is to conceive of the world down-here as being entirely out of reach of any kind of divine being that might interrupt it by means of miracles or other providential activity; the material realm functions strictly according to mechanism, in an entirely regular and predictable manner (we might think of our phrase 'the laws of nature' as a way of encapsulating this idea). But on the other hand, to be modern is also to conceive of the world down-here as being under our control. Engineers, industrialists and medics are able to manipulate and direct the material world in such a way as create bridges, construct steam engines and develop antibiotics. The ideology of modernity therefore posits human beings as *de facto* sovereign agents over the material world. We are the ones who impose order upon nature through our own rational activity. And so within modernity, one form of providence has simply been replaced by another. One master has been removed from the picture (God), only for another immediately to step in and fill the gap (modern, Western, secular people and their institutions).

There can be no doubt that this worldview facilitated the phenomenal development that many societies subsequently experienced. The idea of nature as something that we can observe, control and deploy for our own purposes has been the foundation of the great scientific and technological advances we enjoy and profit from today.

But, as Latour also points out, the ideology of modernity is now coming under strain.[16] At the time of the Anthropocene, we can no longer conceive of the realm of nature as being both *outside ourselves* and *under our control*. We ourselves have become a force altering the material conditions of the environment around us. And the Earth has begun to signal to us its own limits and thereby to threaten the conditions we have hitherto taken for granted, as if it has found its own voice once again. It might even be possible to say that the categories of 'human' and 'nature' themselves, the very categories that had been so carefully differentiated within modernity and that were at the heart of its productive energy, are finding themselves increasingly mixed up at this time.

Modernity has generated the idea that human beings are able to control nature

For some people, then, religion is to blame for the attitudes and behaviours that have led us into the contemporary environmental crisis. But I have suggested that the culprit can be identified closer to home. It is modernity that has generated the idea that human beings are able to observe, control and deploy nature for their own purposes. With the advent of the Anthropocene, however, that relationship will have to be conceived in some other way than it has been up to now. And religion must have some role to play in this process of reconfiguration.

What Assumptions Are We Making as We Respond to the Crisis?

There is no doubt that the shock of the Anthropocene is finally being felt. After a period where scepticism about the effects of environmental change seemed plausible to many, and where some even engaged in outright climate science denial, it now appears that the global community is increasingly mobilizing for some kind of action. The IPCC report, 'Global Warming of 1.5% C,' published in October 2018, has prompted all of us to ask, 'What should we do next?'[17] Individuals, families and institutions are discussing what they can do. The priorities and policy announcements of politicians are slowly shifting in the right direction. All this is very positive and encouraging.

However, if we are to find real and lasting solutions to this crisis, it will not be enough merely to generate a list of action points to follow. We have to think about what has generated the crisis in the first place. And that means getting down to the level of attitudes and ideas. It means being self-aware and even self-critical about the story we have been inhabiting as modern, Western, secular people and about the ways we may be unconsciously replicating that story in our well-meaning attempts to *do the right thing*. It is only when we have done that preliminary work that we will be in a position to avoid duplicating the modernist ideology that got us into this mess in the first place.

We have to think about what has generated the crisis in the first place

It seems to me that some of the solutions to the environmental crisis currently being put forward fail to engage in this preliminary work. This is not to say that they are not worthy of consideration (on the contrary, as I will show, many of them will be absolutely vital and necessary). Nor is it to put into question the benevolent intent of those who are proposing them. But in important ways it seems that some of these proposals have not really grappled with the ideological questions that are underlying the crisis.

As a case study, I would like to introduce a group who define themselves by the name 'ecomodernists.' Amongst their number are found a number of prominent scientists, political activists and writers.[18] Their articles are often featured in magazines and newspaper reports. A recent policy document written by this group has proposed (what is called) a 'Good Anthropocene' strategy.[19] The document was well-received at the time by the Obama administration and has subsequently been influential in many policy-making circles in the United States and elsewhere.

What is the idea that lies behind this strategy? The phrase 'Good Anthropocene' is intended to indicate a positive understanding of the human being, the *anthropos*, as the one who not only generated the crisis in the first place, but through whose initiative and ingenuity that crisis can now be resolved. Proponents of the Good Anthropocene strategy therefore advocate the development and deployment of new technologies and engineering projects as a means of reversing the effects of anthropogenic environmental change. As the document states, the idea is that:

> Human beings should use their growing social, economic and technological powers to make life better for people, to stabilize the climate, and to protect the natural world.[20]

Some of the technologies under consideration include nuclear fusion as an alternative energy resource, the development of super-capacitor batteries for vehicles, and preparation for deliberate and large-scale geoengineering projects designed to sequester carbon from our atmosphere or to manage solar radiation.[21] Significant amounts of funding, including from The Bill and Melinda Gates Foundation and other philanthropic organizations, have already been released to support this research and development, with the aim of bringing some of these technologies to market as soon as possible.[22]

All this sounds very practical and inspiring, of course. Who would not want to make use of the technological and engineering powers we have at our disposal to alleviate (and maybe even reverse) the effects of the environmental crisis?

And yet a potential problem can be identified. For is it not the case that such an approach promotes a trajectory of *more* (not *less*) modernity? The Good Anthropocene strategy offers an optimistic account of the capacity of human beings to resolve the environmental crisis. In doing so, however, it is simply restating the modernist dualism identified above, the human being once again mastering and controlling the realm of nature from the outside and according to their own powers. In fact, part of the intuitive appeal of this strategy is that it presents a utopian promise to human society, allowing us to think that we can continue the trajectory of progress we have enjoyed up to now, albeit with a few technological and engineering fixes added in to maintain the equilibrium and to keep climate change within certain boundaries. It is hardly a surprise, then, that the story told by the Good Anthropocene strategists is proving attractive to the general public. For example, a research paper recently conducted in Sweden analyzed hundreds of news articles and found that one of the most prevalent storylines around the subject of climate change was 'the notion that pure technology is the only possible solution and that it is an adequate substitute for politics.'[23] The Good Anthropocene strategy thus presents itself as a quick fix for all our ills!

And yet the strategy is really nothing but a panacea. It does not prompt us to grapple with the social, economic, political or cultural ideologies that have led to the crisis in the first place. Nor does it challenge us to reconsider the patterns of consumption that are causing that crisis to worsen, not improve, at current rates. As one commentator has recently put it:

> Relying on a technological fix that is just over the horizon avoids the mountain moving required to wean ourselves off fossil fuels, bring hundreds of countries into agreement on how to limit and clean up emissions, and alter the consumption habits of an entire civilization. Those are systemic complexities ingrained in our economies and cultures. Propping up glaciers to limit sea level rise, sprinkling iron dust into the oceans to encourage plankton growth to absorb carbon, or spraying the skies to reflect the sun's heat just seems simpler.[24]

So whilst the Good Anthropocene strategy does indeed seem simpler, it has little to say about the long-term, painstaking, laborious political work that will have to be carried out if the global community is to find a real solution to the challenge it faces. And, as a quick fix, it does not really challenge to us to consider the responsibility we have as individuals to change our behaviour at a deep level. We are not being called to any kind of transformation. We are not being invited to consider the ethical basis for the choices we make or the ideas that may underlie these decisions. We are simply being encouraged to permit science and technology to alleviate the worst effects of the Anthropocene, whilst we carry on the patterns of life to which we have hitherto become accustomed.

5 Can Christianity Offer a Different Story?

Modernity tells us a particular story. If the material world is something that can be observed, controlled and deployed for our own purposes, then there is no reason to doubt that human society can continue on the trajectory of 'progress' we have been enjoying up to now. It is as if we are inhabiting a story where the final chapter is to all extents and purposes known and where we expect no sudden surprises to take place along the way![25] Our strategies to technologize our way out of the crisis can end up as pale reflections of that utopian vision.

But that story is interrupted by the arrival of the Anthropocene. The very air that modern, Western, secular people breathe makes it difficult to conceive of the possibility of a cataclysmic event that will require a wholesale rethink of our lifestyles. And yet, as we have seen, that cataclysmic event is now upon us. As Latour again points out, it is as if the Anthropocene is saying to us, 'Your entire way of life must be modified or else you will disappear as a civilization'![26]

Christians are able to contribute by telling a story into our modern, Western, secular society

Some deeper communication will be needed if we are to meet the challenge of the Anthropocene. It is here that Christianity can enter the scene. On one level, of course, the contribution Christians must make is no different from anyone else: we must alter our practices and change our behaviour on an individual and on a collective level. Many ideas and resources are available to support this activity.[27] But at the same time, Christians can also contribute by telling a story into our modern, Western, secular society. This is a story that can finally begin to reorientate humans towards the action that is required.

An important step towards this is found in the 2015 papal encyclical *Laudato Si'*.[28] This document shows us how Christianity can begin to weave its own story into the surrounding culture at the time of the Anthropocene.

Pope Francis begins the encyclical with words from the canticle of St Francis: 'Praise be to you, my Lord, through our Sister, Mother Earth, who sustains and governs us' (§1).[29] Perhaps this opening sentence might leave us a little cold: is this anything more than a romantic sentiment about the beauties and wonders of nature? But quite the opposite is the case. For Pope Francis immediately goes on to engage this entity, 'Mother Earth,' not merely as an object of contemplation, but as an entity with a voice of her own:

> This sister now cries out to us because of the harm we have inflicted on her by our irresponsible use and abuse of the goods with which God has endowed her. (§1)

By encouraging us to consider the 'cry' of the Earth in this way, the encyclical is challenging the ideology of modernity itself, whose 'tyrannical anthropo-centrism' has caused human beings to look upon nature as mute, inert and subservient to our will (§101, §118). In doing so, it is acknowledging the new world order of the Anthropocene. This is a situation in which anthropocentrism can no longer be sustained. What is needed is an entirely new set of attitudes and ideas governing the relationship of human beings with the world around us.

The encyclical boldly declares that this is where the Christian religion must speak up. For what is needed is nothing less than a 'conversion' of our hearts and minds.[30] And that is part of the great story that Christianity is equipped to tell.

What is needed is nothing less than a 'conversion' of our hearts and minds

It is important to be clear what the encyclical is and is not claiming here. By no means is Pope Francis seeking to undermine secular approaches to the crisis. He urges the development of scientific and technological initiatives to combat environmental degradation (§102 ff). And, quite sensibly, he recognizes the role of political institutions, schools, and other social and community groups in identifying and nurturing environmental values amongst their members wherever possible (§213–214). All these must contribute to the collective action that is required.

Probing Motives

But the encyclical also tentatively probes the motives that lie behind these. To what extent do these initiatives derive from the same ideology that underwrites modernity itself?

> Technology, which…is presented as the only way of solving these problems, in fact proves incapable of seeing the mysterious network of relations between things and so sometimes solves one problem only to create others (§20).

Human initiatives, whether individual or communal, will be counterproductive if there has not first been some kind of alteration or transformation of the human subjects themselves. What is needed, then, is nothing less than the creation of a new ecological citizenship, that is, a population of human beings with an entirely different rationale for action than the one supplied by the ideology of modernity. 'Many things have to change course,' Pope Francis writes, 'but it is we human beings above all who need to change' (§202). In fact, there will have to be a 'profound interior conversion' of humanity itself at the time of the Anthropocene (§217, also §5, §221–226). For him,

> The rich heritage of Christian spirituality, the fruit of twenty centuries of personal and communal experience, has a precious contribution to make to this renewal of humanity (§216).

Saint Francis himself, his spirituality and deeds, are offered as an emblem of this Christian heritage and as an example of why we need to be converted in some way if our relationship with the natural world is to be put on the right footing.[31]

Dislocation between Knowledge and Behaviour

So the encyclical is urging Christians to enter into the public space in order to tell the story that is uniquely theirs. Intriguingly, Pope Francis' approach resonates in interesting ways with what the professionals themselves are asking for at the moment. Frustrated that the climate science itself has apparently been unable to galvanize action, there has recently been recognition amongst the climate science community that their presentation of this issue needs to be rethought. They are increasingly understanding that the dislocation between knowledge and behaviour is not merely the result of an information deficit. Rather, what is needed are ways of embedding the information that climate science provides at a deeper level into our affective, moral and spiritual lives. As Chris Rapley, Professor of Climate Science at University College, London has recently said:

> The science community has spent enormous amounts of effort trying to help you know more. But actually, our task is much harder than that. To tackle climate change, we have to change who people are. We have to give them epiphanies. We have to shift their values and their worldview so that they take this subject seriously and so that they do something about it.[32]

Scientists are wary of straying into this territory, lest they be accused of advocacy. And yet, out of necessity, many scientists and scientific organizations are reaching out to partners to aid them in this task. The Royal Court Theatre in London has recently staged two monologues written by scientists in which these issues are presented in dramatic form.[33] A group of climate scientists under the auspices of the University of Exeter are currently engaging with arts practitioners (song-writers, print-makers and actors) to see how storytelling can be developed as a method to engage the general public on the issue of climate science.[34] Initiatives like these are looking to develop methods of communicating the information that science provides in ways that are engaging, hopeful, actionable and, most of all, experiential.

Christians as Partners

Christians can be partners in this task. After all, we have the ultimate story to tell. We of all people know what it is to have a conversion of the heart and to call others to the same experience and journey. Through the work of George Marshall and others, scientists are becoming aware of what they need to learn from the language of religion.[35] But are we prepared to engage with scientists and others who are inviting our distinctive contribution? Are we emboldened to enter into the public space to contribute to the affective, moral and spiritual conversion that will be needed if we are to find ways to live sustainably at the time of the Anthropocene?

6   What Resources Can Christians Call Upon to Tell Their Story?

There are many places in Scripture that provide us with resources to tell our story. We might refer to the Genesis creation accounts, with their description of the intrinsic value of the entire material world—even apart from its appropriation and cultivation by human beings. We may choose to revisit the biblical theme of covenant, which in Gen 9.12–17 God offers not only to Noah, but to the entire natural order.[36] We might like to draw attention to God's ordination of the Sabbath as an embodied reminder of the sustainable attitudes he calls his people to adopt towards the natural world. As Richard Bauckham puts it:

> The instruction to keep the Sabbath is at least partially about keeping the economic drive in human life within its place and not letting it dominate over the priority to recognize the rights of other created beings to the same resources.[37]

Or we might point to the proclamation of Christ as saviour of the cosmos, whose salvific work extends to the Earth itself and to its entire community of creation.[38]

But there is one resource in particular that we might call upon as we seek to tell our story in the midst of the contemporary culture: the apocalyptic material of Scripture.

The word 'apocalypse' seems to be all around us at the moment. It crops up in media articles and reports that warn us in the strongest possible terms of the threat that climate change poses to us all.[39] Apocalyptic images have been taken up by those working in the visual and plastic arts as a means of communicating the fear that many of us feel as we encounter the data of climate science.[40] Even contemporary film has taken an apocalyptic (or post-apocalyptic) turn in recent years, confronting us with scenarios where humanity has or is about to be overwhelmed by a climatic or other natural disaster.[41]

Throughout history, apocalyptic language has been used at times of societal change

Throughout history, apocalyptic language and imagery has been used at times of societal stress and change. But the word 'apocalypse' does seem strangely appropriate as a means of describing our situation at the time of the Anthropocene. It is as if the challenge posed by the contemporary environmental crisis is so severe, and the requirement that humans change their patterns of behaviour so urgent, that such language alone can attain the necessary register. We might have used the word ourselves in trying to communicate how we feel about environmental matters to those we perceive to be less moved by the issues than ourselves. It seems that even scientists are resorting to such language in their articles and academic reports.[42]

And yet it does not seem that these apocalyptic warnings are having the desired effect. It is as if, having heard the sounding of the alarm, we are still not being roused to action (at least, not with the necessary urgency). This, too, is a function of the ideology of modernity whose effect, as we have seen, is to inculcate in us a quasi-religious belief in the sure and certain forward trajectory of history. Is it really the case that everything we have come to take for granted in our lives is about to change? Surely something or someone will come to our rescue, and things will continue much as before? And so the word apocalypse has been emptied of meaning: modern, Western, secular people find it hard to conceive of a future that might look substantially different from the present. What results is a curious incapacity for action and a tendency to emotional withdrawal when faced with the severity of the issues that confront us.

The Trajectory of History

Christians, however, can redeem the meaning of apocalypse by telling a different story about the trajectory of history. We have a resource to do this in the apocalyptic material of Scripture. This might sound like a strange move to make. For some, the thrust of biblical apocalyptic is to close down or negate a sense of agency in the present moment. If the future is already set, and is revealed to us by God himself, then what can we do here on Earth that is of enduring value or that might contribute to permanent change?

And yet, the apocalyptic material of Scripture functions in quite the opposite way. To demonstrate this, let me propose three general statements about the nature and function of this genre:

1   The apocalyptic material in Scripture serves to temporarily reveal or disclose a future state of affairs.

2   But it does so in such a way as to remind us that this state of affairs still lies in the future and is not the reality we see around us now.

3   Therefore, precisely because this material deals with a not-yet, its function is to prompt and inspire new or renewed forms of action in the present moment.

The apocalyptic material in Scripture does indeed draw back the curtain on a state of affairs that is yet to come. But precisely by showing us that this future is not-yet, its function is to send us back into the world with energy and resolve to play our part in an unfolding narrative. The drawing back of the curtain enacted within this genre prompts us to become newly-responsible agents within the flow of history, emboldened and empowered to get involved in the social, cultural and political arenas we occupy right now. We have faith in God to redeem and heal the world at the end of history. But this inspires us to involve ourselves in the drama that is unfolding with us in its midst.

What a contrast this provides with the narrative of modernity, with its implied requirement that we must passively acquiesce to a trajectory that has been already set for us from above. By retrieving this sense of the biblical genre, the paralysis of modernity under which we currently labour can be broken. The word 'apocalypse' can be rescued from its banal appropriation to become instead the catalyst for the sort of affective, moral and spiritual transformation that is needed at the time of the Anthropocene.

Holding Back Lawlessness

An example of this can be found in 2 Thess 2.1–10. In that passage, we discover that rumours had been circulating among the Christian community in Thessalonica concerning the imminent return of Jesus Christ, generated (it seems) by a letter purporting to have been written by the apostle Paul himself. In response, Paul offers some instruction on the end times. He reminds the Christian community in Thessalonica that first of all 'the man of lawlessness' has to be revealed, 'the one who opposes' Christ and his followers. This adversary is 'already at work' in the world. But his impact is being held under check by a force or power that 'restrains it.' Only when this restraining effect is removed will the final confrontation between the man of lawlessness and Christ take place, with the triumph of Christ then being followed by the end of history itself. So what are we to make of this restraining force or power? Much ink has been spilt on the interpretation of these verses.[43] For Tertullian, this restraining force or power was to be identified with the Roman Empire (for which he entreated all Christians to pray earnestly).[44] But for Augustine, it was God himself who was holding back the end of

These verses provide a powerful motivation for Christians to engage in the world around us

time so as to give opportunity for more people to be converted and come to faith.[45] These verses therefore provided a powerful motivation for Christians to engage in the world around them as salt and light, knowing that the time is *now* to make a difference.

Christianity tells a story powerful enough to break the spell of modernity. It is as if Christians alone have an understanding of history that can inspire us to make a difference now. Because the end is at the end, held in abeyance by God himself, the present becomes the site of real, consequential and purposeful activity. And, as a result, we can convey the Christian quality of hope to the world, a hope for the future that is grounded not in our own ingenuity to make things right, but in the call of God that we should be agents of change here and now.[46]

Naturally, it is not always easy to translate the Christian story into our contemporary context. Christians will need to discern the situations into which they can speak. But by telling this story and, more importantly, by living it out, Christians will be able to respond faithfully to the crisis that faces us at the time of the Anthropocene.

7

Conclusion

A new kind of thinking is needed at the time of the Anthropocene. Many of the assumptions associated with the ideology of modernity, with its utopian promise of an endless trajectory of progress, can no longer be sustained. Political co-operation is proving difficult to achieve. Human beings are feeling deanimated in the presence of the huge challenges that face us, as if we do not know how to reconcile our desire to act with the hard choices demanded of us personally and communally. A fundamental change of orientation is needed.

It is into this breach that Christians can contribute a new kind of story. Our faith gives us the resources to react to the new epoch that is represented by the Anthropocene. For us, history is in the hands of a sovereign God. As Isaiah 35.4 reminds us, we really do have nothing to fear. But it is precisely because the end is at the end that the present time can be envisaged as a moment for real action, that is, for action that can really make a difference. The God who lies *outside* history calls us to become agents *within* history. It is when Christians synchronize these two things that we will be able to offer something constructive and essential to global society at the time of the Anthropocene.

Notes

1   M R Hodson and M J Hodson, *The Ethics of Climatic Scepticism* (Grove Ethics book-
    let E177); M R Hodson and M J Hodson, *An Introduction to Environmental Ethics*
    (Grove Ethics booklet E184).

2   For more information on the subcommission and its work, see http://quaternary.
    stratigraphy.org (accessed 08 October 2018).

3   W Steffen, J Grinevald, P Crutzen and J McNeill, 'The Anthropocene: Conceptual
    and Historical Perspectives' in *Philosophical Transactions of the Royal Society A*,
    2011, No 369, p 843.

4   W F Ruddiman, 'The Anthropogenic Greenhouse Era Began Thousands of Years
    Ago' in *Climate Science*, 2003, No 61, pp 261–293. For a response to criticisms of
    the hypothesis, see W F Ruddiman, 'The Early Anthropogenic Hypothesis: Chal-
    lenges and Responses' in *Reviews of Geophysics*, 2007, No 45, pp 1–37.

5   P J Crutzen and E F Stoermer, 'The Anthropocene' in *Global Change: Newsletter of
    the International Geosphere-Biosphere Programme*, 2000, No 41, pp 17–18.

6   For a brief overview of some of these claims, see C Hamilton and J Grinevald, 'Was
    the Anthropocene Anticipated?' in *The Anthropocene Review*, 2015, Vol 2, No 1,
    pp 59–72.

7   For more on the methodology and implications of their decision, see P Warde, L
    Robin and S Sörlin, 'Stratigraphy for the Renaissance: Questions of Expertise for
    "the Environment" and "the Anthropocene"' in *The Anthropocene Review*, 2017,
    Vol 4, No 3, pp 246–258.

8   An ongoing project at the Australian National University is attempting to monitor
    public and media discourse about the concept of the Anthropocene, for which
    see http://cpas.anu.edu.au/research/projects/anthropocene-media (accessed 8
    October 2018).

9   Y Martel, *Life of Pi: A Novel* (London: Canongate, 2001); *Life of Pi* (director: Ang
    Lee, 2012).

10 L White Jr, 'The Historical Roots of our Ecologic Crisis' in *Science*, 1967, Vol 155,
    No 3767, pp 1203–1207.

11 *ibid*, p 1205.

12 For a survey of responses to the article in the years since its publication, see E
    Whitney, 'Lynn White Jr's *The Historical Roots of Our Ecologic Crisis* after Fif-
    ty Years' in *History Compass*, 2017, Vol 13, No 8, pp 396–410.

13 For a detailed analysis of the pre-modern mind in precisely these terms, see M S
    Northcott, *A Political Theology of Climate Change* (Grand Rapids, MI: Eerdmans,
    2013) p 22 ff.

14 For a study of the development of modernity in precisely these terms, see S
    Gaukroger, *The Emergence of a Scientific Culture: Science and the Shaping of
    Modernity 1210–1685* (Oxford University Press, 2006).

15 See especially B Latour, *We Have Never Been Modern*, C Porter (trans) (Cambridge, MA: Harvard University Press, 1993).

16 See especially B Latour, *Facing Gaia: Eight Lectures on the New Climatic Regime*, C Porter (trans) (London: Polity Press, 2017).

17 IPCC special report on the impacts of global warming above 1.5% C, October 2018, available at http://www.ipcc.ch/report/sr15 (accessed 17 October 2018).

18 Prominent among these are writers such as David Keith, Erle Ellis and Mark Lynas. For a general study of their approach, see C Isenhour, 'Unearthing Human Progress? Ecomodernism and Contrasting Definitions of Technological Progress in the Anthropocene' in *Economic Anthropology*, 2016, Vol 3, No 2, pp 315–328.

19 M Shellenberger and T Nordhaus, 'The Ecomodernist Manifesto,' available at www.ecomodernism.org (accessed 12 October 2018).

20 *ibid.*

21 See O Morton, *The Planet Remade: How Geo-engineering Could Change the World* (Princeton, NJ: Princeton University Press, 2017).

22 This has taken place through the Breakthrough Energy Coalition, for which see http://www.b-t.energy.com (accessed 17 October 2018).

23 J Anshelm and A Hansson, 'The Last Chance to Save the Planet? An Analysis of the Geoengineering Advocacy Discourse in the Public Debate' in *Environmental Humanities*, 2014, Vol 5, No 1, pp 101–123.

24 A Bajak, 'The Dangerous Belief That Extreme Technology Will Fix Climate Change,' available at www.huffingtonpost.com/geoengineering-climate-change (accessed 21 November 2018).

25 It is no coincidence that at the turn of the century some Western intellectuals proposed (what they called) 'the end of history.' See F Fukuyama, *The End of History and the Last Man* (New York: Simon and Schuster, 2006).

26 B Latour, 'Will Non-Humans be Saved? An Argument in Ecotheology' in *The Journal of the Royal Anthropological Institute*, 2009, Vol 15, No 3, pp 459–475, here p 462.

27 A useful place to begin is R Valerio, *Just Living: Faith and Community in an Age of Consumerism* (London: Hodder and Stoughton, 2016) especially part 3.

28 Pope Francis, *Encyclical Letter Laudato Si': On Care for our Common Home* (London: Catholic Truth Society, 2015).

29 Citing 'Canticle of the Creatures' in R J Armstrong (ed), *Francis of Assisi: Early Documents, Volume 1* (New York: New City Press, 1999) pp 113–114.

30 For technical analysis of the use of the word 'conversion' in the encyclical, see T Howles, J Reader and M J Hodson, '"Creating an Ecological Citizenship": Philosophical and Theological Perspectives on the Role of Contemporary Environmental Education' in *Heythrop Journal*, 2018, Vol 59, No 6, pp 997–1008.

31 For the significance of the ideas of Francis of Assisi on the theology of the encyclical, see K W Irwin, *A Commentary on* Laudato Si': *Examining the Background, Contributions, Implementation and Future of Pope Francis' Encyclical* (New York: Paulist Press, 2016) pp 32–36. For an interesting comparative study, see W B

Hurlbut, 'St. Francis, Christian Love, and the Biotechnological Future' in *The New Atlantis*, 2013, No 38, pp 93–100.

32 C Rapley, 'Communicating Climate Change: Why So Toxic?' a lecture given at the London School of Economics (LSE) on 30 October 2018, available at www.lse. ac.uk/lse-player?id=4540 (accessed 28 November 2018).

33 *Ten Billion*, by Stephen Emmott (12 July–11 August 2012); *2071*, by Chris Rapley and Duncan Macmillan (30 November 2014–24 January 2015). The script for the latter is available in C Rapley and D Macmillan, *2071: The World We'll Leave our Grandchildren* (London: John Murray, 2015).

34 *The Climate Stories* project, Principal Investigator Professor Peter Stott, funded by a Natural Environment Research Council grant no NE/R011729/1.

35 For example G Marshall, 'What the Climate Movement must learn from Religion,' *The Guardian*, available at www.theguardian.com/commentisfree/2015/apr/04/ climate-change-campaigners-evangelism-religion-activism (accessed 25 November 2018).

36 D G Horrell, *The Bible and the Environment: Towards a Critical Ecological Biblical Theology* (Abingdon: Routledge, 2010) especially chapter 4, 'The Fall and the Flood: A Covenant with all the Earth,' pp 37–48.

37 R Bauckham, *The Bible and Ecology: Rediscovering the Community of Creation* (London: Darton, Longman and Todd, 2010) p 19.

38 D G Horrell, *op cit*, especially chapter 6, 'Jesus and the Earth: The Gospels and Ecology,' pp 62–73.

39 C Green, 'Apocalyptic threat: dire climate report raises fears for California's future,' *The Guardian*, available at www.theguardian.com/environment/2018/ aug/27/california-climate-change-report-wildfires-jerry-brown (accessed 28 November 2018).

40 For representations of apocalypse in art and other visual media, see H Davis and E Turpin (eds), *Art in the Anthropocene: Encounters Among Aesthetics, Politics, Environments and Epistemologies* (London: Open Humanities Press, 2015).

41 For example, see *Melancholia* (director: Lars Von Trier, 2011) or *The Turin Horse* (directors: Béla Tarr and Ágnes Hranitzky, 2011). These recent films can be contrasted with a series of Hollywood productions from the 1990s: whilst these centred on the threat of a world-destroying disaster of some sort, that threat would ultimately be resolved through the action of some individual hero (usually Bruce Willis) or combined national effort (usually led by the President of the United States). This reflected an understanding that the coming environmental crisis would most likely be manageable through private or intergovernmental action.

42 For a useful survey of the prevalence of apocalyptic language in the natural sciences, see D C Rose, 'Five Ways to Enhance the Impact of Climate Science' in *Nature Climate Change*, 2014, No 4, pp 522–524.

43 For a survey of interpretations of these verses among early Christian writers, see F Witt Hughes, *Early Christian Rhetoric and 2 Thessalonians* (Sheffield: Continuum, 1989).

44 Tertullian, *Apologetic Works*, chapter 32, section 1, p 88, J Daly and E A Quain (trans) (Washington, DC: Catholic University of America Press, 1997).

45 Augustine, *City of God*, 20.19 in P Schaff (ed), *Nicene and Post-Nicene Fathers: First Series, Volume II* (New York: Cosimo, 2007).

46 For a detailed exploration of the Christian theme of hope in relation to the contemporary environment crisis, see the special edition of *Anvil: Anglican Evangelical Journal for Theology and Mission* Vol 29, Issue 1 (September 2013). See especially J Weaver, 'Exploring Hope,' pp 25–41 and R Bauckham, 'Ecological Hope in Crisis,' pp 43–54.